CYBERSENSE

THE LEADER'S GUIDE TO PROTECTING CRITICAL INFORMATION

By

Prof. Derek Smith

"The Worlds #1 Cybersecurity Expert"

Speaker, Author, Writer, Educator

National Cybersecurity Education Center Publishing

Bowie, MD

HELP OTHERS TO PROTECT THEIR CRITICAL INFORMATION!

"Share This Book"

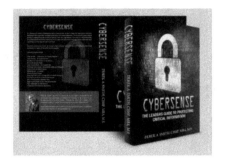

Retail for $19.95

Quantity discounts available!

To place an order contact:

info@NCSEConline.com

THE IDEAL PROFESSIONAL SPEAKER FOR YOUR NEXT EVENT

Any organization that wants to develop their people's knowledge of cybersecurity needs to hire Derek for a keynote and/or workshop training!

TO CONTACT OR BOOK DEREK TO SPEAK OR TRAIN:

National Cybersecurity Education Center

www.ncseconline.com

301 744-7355

derek@ncseonline.com

Copyright ©2017 National Cybersecurity Education Center

Disclaimer: This book is solely for educational purposes and should be used as an educational tool only. The author takes no responsibility for any misappropriation of the content of this book and, thus, cannot be held liable for any damages of any kind incurred due to the content of the book. The author or publisher does not warrant the absolute accuracy of the content and denies all responsibility for the information contained in the book, its accuracy, and application. The advice in this book may not be suitable for all persons and is not a substitute for personal professional advice and should not be taken as such. The author or publisher does not endorse any person that is quoted in this book. Please note that individual results may vary when implementing the information in this book, and the author or publisher is not responsible for the results.

First Edition

ISBN-9781499128154

Dedication

This book is dedicated to my wife Andrea, my wonderful daughters Jaime, and the twins Mackenzie and Madison. I thank the many people that made this book possible by providing me with experiences and the knowledge needed to build my cybersecurity career.

Contents

Introduction

Today, any leader who is not concerned about the cybersecurity of their business or organization is simply neglecting their due diligence in protecting the organization. Prudence demands that cybersecurity is essential for every forward-thinking leader. Cybersecurity is no longer optional for *any* organization, and leaders must usher in and understand advance cybersecurity to prevent data compromise.

The costly problem of data breaches is not going away anytime soon. Stolen data equals big money for cybercriminals. Any information and technologies asset that provides rewards/money with minimum effort is vulnerable. In fact, The Identity Theft Resource Center says that, according to their mid-year report, "The number of U.S. data breaches tracked through June 30, 2017, hit a half-year record high of 791 (Identity Theft Resource Center 2017). The ITRC says they anticipate the number of breaches could reach 1,500 in 2017, which would be a 37 percent annual increase over 2016.

Cybercriminals are not just passing through. They are setting up camp and improving their technologies. Leaders must do the same. They no longer have the option of hiding behind fear of technology and the lack of understanding of cybersecurity. Procrastination and thinking that *someday* you'll get around to taking a course and learning what must be done to protect your business has been the devastating mistake that many leaders have made to the demise of their business.

Today is the day to get the education you need regarding cybersecurity, and this book is the start of understanding the benefits and implementation of cybersecurity for your business. Every day that you put off the responsibility of cybersecurity is another day that your organization is vulnerable.

Cybersense—The Leader's Guide to Protecting Critical Information is a comprehensive guide written by Derek Smith, the Worlds #1 Cybersecurity Expert, that contains critical and practical information for helping leaders devise strategies to protect their company from data compromise. This guide answers the following questions and many others for which all leaders need answers:

- Exactly what is cybersecurity?
- Why is cybersecurity important to my organization?
- Is my business a good candidate for cybersecurity measures?
- How can I protect my organization from data compromise?
- How can I continually monitor the security of my organization's data with constant cyber threats occurring?
- How can I implement cybersecurity quickly and efficiently?

Leaders do not leave any other critical systems in their organization vulnerable to attack. Why would they leave information assets and technologies vulnerable when there is a simple solution to the vulnerability? Fear of the unknown may contribute to the hesitation to move forward with cybersecurity. It is important to note that cybersecurity has now become the responsibility of leaders. It is no longer reserved for the behind-the-scenes techies and geeks. Leaders need a firm understanding of how they can best protect their organization whether they are the Chief Information Security Officer for the organization or are required to work closely with the CISO. Effective leaders must be proactive to learn what they need to know.

This guide provides up-to-date information in an ever-changing industry. It is written by a trusted industry leader who understands what you need to know most about cybersecurity and provides that information in a format that is easy to grasp, taking away any excuse for ignoring cyber security and leaving your business vulnerable.

Take the first step in minimizing your organization's vulnerability by reading this book. It may be one of the best business decisions you'll ever make.

"Security is a business issue, not a technical one."

T. Glaesnner

1: Why Leaders Must Take Cybersecurity Seriously

On any given day, if you read or listen to the major media reports, you are aware that politicians, celebrities, retailers, corporations, small businesses, financial institutions, and individuals suffer at the hands of sophisticated and determined cybercriminals that illegally gain access to important private and confidential information.

The cybercriminals use the information they steal in many ways. One of the most common and dangerous ways the stolen data is used is for phishing frauds. Because the data thief has access to your name, address, phone number, social security number and other personal, sensitive information, they can use that information to call you or email you with the hope of getting more information that gives them unauthorized access to your bank accounts and credit card accounts.

The hackers can also use the stolen information against the individual or organization or sell it to competitors or identity thieves for personal gain. Most organizations are targeted for financial gain while others face advanced persistent attacks for such activities as political power or as leverage for a specific movement, cause, or organization.

Cyberattacks are also launched as a form of revenge. An organization may involuntarily become entrenched in a dark tale of employee vengeance, unscrupulous competitors, those who have a point to make, or others who seek revenge.

Some organizations seem to be targeted by hackers who hack businesses for no reason other than to create chaos and misfortune for the company.

The major Target (the data breach of November 2013 is an example of a cyberattack where millions of customers' names, addresses, credit card information, bank account information, and other private information were compromised.

Such reports have become so common that, likely, if the data breach does not personally affect you and your information, you may do what most Americans do—shrug your shoulders and ask why those smart hackers can't find something productive to do. Most feel somewhat powerless to escape the brutal effects of such attacks completely but do very little to become educated about how to protect themselves or their company if they are in a leadership position and ultimately responsible for the security of the company.

Meanwhile, cybercriminals are highly productive, working around the clock to stay one step ahead of business leaders who sleep on the job of making sure their company's critical information, intellectual property, financial records, and customer information is secure. While leaders are using outdated technology and ignoring security, cybercriminals are utilizing the latest technology to get their job done. In fact, in the Target data breach, analysts have pointed out that the breach could have been prevented at different points prior to the breach happening if some of the following issues had been given the proper attention and security measures taken: too much accessible preliminary information available; compromised third-party vendor; vendor portal access; malware detection alarm not heeded; vulnerability in servers; and point of sale system malware (Kassner 2015).

Again, cybercriminals are sophisticated and determined. They know what they want and know how to find it within your organization if security is not optimal. Yet, many small and medium-size businesses trust their data security to someone who does not understand cybersecurity. In many instances, the owner or manager is responsible for data security, which is fine *if* the owner or manager is well educated in data security matters and understands what security is needed and how to implement and constantly monitor it. At the very least, leaders in charge of cyber security must understand their vulnerabilities; how to keep technology updated as needed; the best software for monitoring the latest types of cyberattacks; what their vital role is in protecting their company from an external cyberattack or an internal attack; and how to secure their own personal devices such as cell phones and laptops that are used for business purposes.

When a cyberattack directly affects you and your organization, the damage is too great to simply shrug your shoulders and grumble about cybercriminals. After an attack happens, it's too late to take preventive measures.

As the leader of your company, you may be aware of some of the threats and risks your business and many other businesses face because critical data is stored on cloud computing and online networks and databases. What you may not realize is just how vulnerable your business is and the extent of damage that can be done by the lack of adequate cybersecurity. The objective of this chapter is to help you understand that cybersecurity is of the utmost importance to your business and why you cannot afford to ignore it if you intend to compete in the marketplace.

If you don't understand why it is critical for you to understand cybersecurity so that you can implement and monitor it, rest assured that your organization is vulnerable to financial damage, loss of trustworthiness in the marketplace, loss of loyal customer base, and may be liable for damages.

Financial Damage

For the Ponemon Institute's "2016 Cost of Data Breach Study: Global Analysis," 383 organizations that endured at least one breach in 2016 were queried, and the average cost per breach was found to be $4 million globally and $7 million in the United States (Laberis 2016).

You may think that your business is small and, therefore, not a significant target for data breaches and cybercrime. Even if your business is small, the percentage of dollars lost to cybercrime can be proportionately devastating to the company. In fact, a Small Business Trends article, "Cyber Security Statistics—Numbers Small Businesses Need to Know" states that 43 percent of cyberattacks target small businesses, and 60 percent of small companies go out of business within six months of a cyberattack (Mansfield 2017). The same article says that only 14 percent of small businesses rate their ability to mitigate cyber risks, vulnerabilities, and attacks as highly effective.

Every year millions of dollars in revenue are lost to cyber security breaches. Large corporations that have money to throw at cyberattacks in the form of cyber liability insurance may endure one or multiple attacks, but most small to medium businesses will not survive a major attack that affects their integral data. This may be especially true for fledgling start-up businesses that are trying to get their feet on solid business ground.

Small to medium businesses may be the preferred target of even some of the most sophisticated cybercriminals. Why wouldn't cybercriminals go where the big money is? The cybercriminals understand that small to medium-sized businesses are the least likely to have stringent security in place to stop the attack. They also know that smaller organizations do not always have the staff to stay on top of security and that leaders do not understand how to direct staff for optimum security. Additionally, they understand that small and medium businesses are less likely to invest huge sums of money to track down the criminals after the attack. It is kind of the same mentality that old-fashioned bank robbers had: There is a lot more money in the vault at the big city bank, but the small-town bank is much easier to rob.

Many small retail businesses are vulnerable to hackers that want access to customers' credit card or bank information. In this case, the cybercriminal may use the information to steal from the customers' accounts, or they may encrypt the stolen information and hold it hostage until the business pays them a requested amount of money. Because the business leader has often failed to back up the information properly, they have no choice but to pay the hackers for the retrieval of the information.

According to the "2016 State of SMB Cybersecurity Report," half of the 28 million small businesses in the U.S. were hacked in a twelve-month period.

Trust, Branding, and Customer Retention Damage

In addition to the financial damage that can be caused by security breaches and stolen data, there is a trust and branding issue that presents itself after a data breach is announced. Most businesses invest time and marketing dollars into building trust with their customers and making their brand known. This may be particularly true of online businesses since many people are recently coming to terms with online business and security. Once this trust is compromised, customers may look elsewhere for a *trustworthy* business that they can have faith in regarding their information. Customers are only loyal to the extent that they can trust a business.

Customers have the expectation that the information they provide your company, everything from their email address, credit card information, social security number, financial information to the orders they place is confidential and will never extend beyond the office of your company. They have the expectation that the company can be trusted to eliminate or mitigate cyber risks. Any leader who fails to do so can become a sitting duck for cybercriminals and the aftermath of an attack. Knowing that loyal customers are the heartbeat of your business, can you afford to take such a risk with your loyal customers?

It is costly in time, effort, and the marketing budget for a business to try to gain back loyal customers once the customers have decided to go elsewhere; not to mention the fact that, once a customer leaves the business for breach of trust and confidence, the customer may be highly unlikely to return to that business.

Employees, business partners, and investors also have the expectation that you can be trusted to keep sensitive information secure and private. It is also betraying their trust when the business is unnecessarily vulnerable to cybersecurity risks.

Liability

The data stored on company computers and transferred through emails, texts, and messaging creates a digital fingerprint that can be used by hackers and other parties with malicious intent to obtain information about you, employees, and the company. In some instances, if this information is funneled into the wrong hands, the company's failure to take reasonable and expected measures to protect their customers' and employees' information can create a serious liability for the company.

When business and manufacturing processes are stopped due to security issues, contracts with customers may be broken, and products may not be available as promised to customers. This can also create liability issues.

Your business is constantly under the watchful eye of cybercriminals. To know this and do little or nothing about it puts your company at risk for liability issues.

Cybersecurity knowledge is necessary for any leader that wants to establish or maintain their trusted standing in the marketplace, retain their loyal customers, and grow their business without the damage that can be incurred with successful cyberattacks.

2: Cybercriminals and Cybercrime

Who are the Cybercriminals?

For some, *cybercriminals* and *cybercrime* are mysterious terms and conjure up hoody-wearing, pimple-faced geeks who stay up all night in the basement of their parents' home, finding entertainment in hacking people's email and Facebook accounts. That is, however, the criminal of yesteryear. That image does not necessarily fit the sophisticated cybercriminals that have the capability to shut down multi-million-dollar businesses.

Cybercriminals are often businessmen and businesswomen in the sense that they launch cyberattacks to get something that is far more valuable to them than sheer entertainment. It is how they make their living. In other words, they are serious about what they do, and they do it well.

Cyberthieves may be silent thieves walking among you—your neighbor, co-worker, a teller at your neighborhood bank, or the cashier at the supermarket. Many cybercriminals maintain day jobs as part of their front for what they really do.

It is not highly unusual for a model employee who becomes disgruntled with the company for reasons such as being passed over for a promotion or being humiliated in front of coworkers to turn to cybercriminal activity for revenge. The employee may have access to sensitive and proprietary files that he or she can turn over to competitors for monetary gain or for the sheer pleasure of seeing the company suffer.

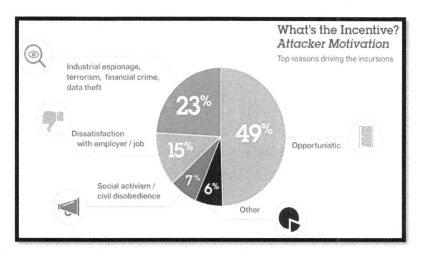

Source: The 2013 IBM Cyber Security Index

Cybercriminals may be motivated by one of the several factors or a combination of factors, including intolerance of certain groups; political beliefs; desire for control and manipulation; religious beliefs; to prove they are intelligent; thrill-seeking; attention-seeking; financial gain; espionage or sabotage; dissatisfaction with job or leadership; social activism; reputation among cybercriminals; and just because they are bored, and they have the skill set to do something that is challenging.

Cybercriminals may be novices that are just out to have some fun and shake up some people, then realize they are good at what they do. They may continue to learn and develop the skills needed to do serious damage and make money with what started out as a hobby.

Many cybercriminals work in technical positions and develop skills on the job that are later used, ironically, against the company that trained them.

Here is a closer look at three specific types of common cybercriminals:

- **Hackers**—Hackers are those who find the act of accessing restricted data exhilarating and enjoyable. These people may "hack" systems for the pure joy that it brings them to overcome the challenge before them. Sometimes, hackers are hired by companies to "test" their systems for vulnerabilities.
- **Hacktivists**—Hacktivists are hackers who are also activists. They may be an activist for a political, animal welfare, religious, ecological, or human rights cause, among others. Their goal is to protect something, right a wrong, or bring awareness to the public about issues that they feel strongly about. Sometimes hacktivists access a company's information to expose the company's policies on certain issues or to harm the company's reputation because they believe the company is harmful to their cause.
- **Employees**—Employees may knowingly or unknowingly access confidential information that is critical for business operations. In some cases,

competitive businesses may even send a spy to your company to pose as an employee to infiltrate your defense system.

Additionally, disgruntled employees may find it gives them a sense of power to know they can access confidential information and use it against the company or senior leadership in a company.

- **Industry Competitors**—Industry competitors may find it worth their while to hack your system to gain industry secrets or other information that could help them defeat you if you are a leading competitor. Again, spies masquerading as employees may be sent to your company to sabotage your business.

- **Financial Gain**—Many cybercriminals work individually or as a group for financial gain. They may get no personal satisfaction out of the work but do it simply because they can do the work for financial gain. These individuals and groups may steal customer credit card information; transfer funds from a customer's bank account to their own account; use credit card numbers and accompanying personal information to charge expensive purchases for themselves or take expensive vacations, or open new accounts in their name using someone else's credit information.

Knowing the different types of cybercriminals can help you know what you are up against and how to best strategize to protect your company. It's always good to know who your enemy is!

What is Cybercrime and How Did It Start?

Cybercrime has become mainstream and transcends all industries. Now, mostly, instead of gun-wielding masked bank robbers holding up banks for cash, computers, phones, and other devices that connect online are used to rob companies of their money or the information required for the criminals to get money from hundreds, thousands, or even millions of customers. Criminals who may be reluctant to hold a gun and physically rob a business may feel quite comfortable stealing money, credit card numbers, or identities with their specialized software and few swift strokes on the keyboard.

Cybercrime is a not a new development. In 1971, John Draper committed wire fraud when he built a device with a whistle that gained him access to the telephone switching computers and allowed him to make free long-distance phone calls.

In 1981 Ian Murphy was the first person to be convicted of a cybercrime when he hacked into the AT&T network and changed the internal clock to charge the off-hours rate for peak time usage.

After the *War Games* movie, in which a teenager hacked into a government computer, was released in the early 80s, more people became aware of hacking. By 1986, hacking was enough of a problem that Congress passed the Computer Fraud and Abuse Act that declared hacking and theft as an illegal activity.

After the World Wide Web was launched in 1994, hackers had a new worldwide playground with the launching of websites. Soon, hackers were hacking into NASA and government systems using their Commodore computers. While most people were figuring out how to navigate the World Wide Web, cybercriminals were figuring out how to use it to accomplish what they wanted.

By the mid-to-late 90s, macro-viruses (viruses written in computer code and embedded in applications and are launched when the application is opened) were rampant. Foreign-based crime rings constantly tried to hack the US government networks, and many US companies were victims of money transfers at the hands of hackers. Criminals had found an in-road to unlawfully achieving their goals.

The advent of social media, where people store a gold-mine of personal information online, was yet another lucrative break for cybercriminals.

Throughout the late 90s and on until present, cybercriminals have managed to stay a step ahead of solutions for the criminal activity. The crimes committed have only become more sophisticated and are executed with precision and speed, making it difficult to quickly identify and stop an attack. Nonetheless, when the leader of a company understands cybersecurity and makes sure preventive measures and alerts are in place, the cybercriminals have a lower success rate.

According to Technopedia, "Cybercrime is defined as a crime in which a computer is the object of the crime (hacking, phishing, spamming) or is used as a tool to commit an offense (child pornography, gain access to ransom money, and hate crimes). Cybercriminals may use computer technology to access personal information, business trade secrets or use the internet for exploitive or malicious purposes" (Technopedia n.d.).

According to the same article cited above, cybercrime can be divided into two main categories:

- Crimes that use computer networks to carry out other criminal activities such as phishing, fraud, identity theft, and cyberstalking
- Crimes that directly target computer networks or devices such as cell phones with viruses and denial-

of-service attacks, rendering the computer or device locked or useless.

Types of Cyber Attacks

Leaders may not be aware of the many ways that cyberthieves can infiltrate and cause harm to their company. Here is a short list of some of the most common ways that individuals and businesses can be affected by cyberattacks. There are several other avenues that cybercriminals take to infiltrate systems and steal from companies.

- **Phishing**—Phishing attacks are sent to a company or individual within the company through email. Usually, the email contains a live link that the email recipient is requested to click on for a specific purpose. For instance, the email may state that the company needs to update their credit card information with a vendor and can do so by simply clicking on the link and providing the requested information. Since the email looks legitimate, the email recipient may automatically click on the link and provide sensitive information. However, the information does not go to the intended vendor. Instead, the information has been typed into a dummy site that directs the information to the cybercriminal where it can be used for identity theft to open credit card and other credit accounts or to access bank accounts and other accounts. If the cyberthief has access to personal information, they can quickly do a great deal of harm to your company.

- **Man-in-the-Middle (MITM)**—With the Man-in-the-Middle (MITM) attack is used to collect information from you and from the person you are communicating with. As an example, if you bank at Bank of America, the Man-in-the-Middle attacker would gain control of the communication between you and Bank of America through a vulnerable non-encrypted wireless access point. Then, represent you to Bank of America and represent Bank of America to you. Therefore, they would gain all information from both parties and collect the sensitive information needed for access to bank accounts, etc.

- **Rogue Software**—Rogue software usually comes in the form of pop-up windows and alerts. The pop-ups and alerts suddenly flash a caution sign on the screen and tell you the computer or device is infected or some such message. The pop-ups look legitimate and tell the computer or device user that they must download security software to keep the computer or device safe. When the user clicks on the link to say "yes" to download the software, the malware is downloaded onto the device or computer.

- **Cracking Passwords**—Cracking passwords seems like such an elementary game for cybercriminals to play, but the truth is, if the thieves have access to your passwords to accounts, they can manipulate your accounts for their malicious purposes and do extended damage to your company.

- **Malware**—Malware is code that is sent to your computer, often through email attachments or software downloads, with the malicious intent to steal data or destroy files on the computer. Worms, viruses, and trojans are common forms of malware.

- **Malvertising**—Malvertising is when cyber attackers upload enticing ads that are infected with malware. When you click on the ad, the malware is downloaded to your system.

- **Drive-By Downloads**—Drive-by Downloads can happen when there are vulnerabilities in your operating system or programs such as Adobe, and you visit an otherwise legitimate website that has code for malware.

- **Denial-of-Service (DoS) Attacks**—Denial-of-Service attacks, also known as DoS attacks are launched to render the affected network unusable. A high volume of data or traffic is sent through the network so the network becomes overloaded and cannot function. This type of attack is often used by groups or individuals who want to make a point to large organizations or the government.

Because cybercrimes have been well-established over the past few decades, you might think that cybersecurity would be a high priority for every business leader. Sadly, that is not the case. Many business leaders exclaim that they simply do not understand enough about cybersecurity to protect their company. There are many types of cyberattacks, and the cybercriminals seem to be working overtime all the time. Fortunately, a leader can take effective steps to keep their company from so easily becoming prey to the cybercriminals.

3: Cybersecurity Knowledge Is the Leader's Responsibility

In the previous chapters, you learned that cyberattacks are at an all-time high level and frequency, and no business is one-hundred percent immune to the disruption of business caused by cybercriminals. This fact alone means every business is vulnerable simply because the business uses wireless technology.

You also learned that cybercriminals are productive and knowledgeable enough about technology to constantly roll out new types of attacks, particularly against companies that leave open doors for cybercriminals to enter the business, including small businesses and huge corporations. It's apparent that no business can afford to ignore cybersecurity without creating tremendous risk and possibly the failure of the company to thrive or survive.

But it's not all bad news on the cybersecurity front. A capable leader can mitigate the risks and effects of malicious cyber activity by implementing preventive measures, detecting malicious activity, and responding to the activity in a timely and effective manner.

The Manager's Role in Cybersecurity

Anyone who is a manager understands there are many definitions for the word *manager*. You also know that business managers for most organizations wear many different hats. This is especially true for small organizations. Managers are directly involved with overseeing the day-to-day operations of a business and providing support to his or her assigned department or area. Managers also report to their superiors and serve as a liaison between senior management and staff. All the manager's duties, in one way or another, lead to productively helping the business productively function for the profit, growth, and success of the company.

Primarily, managers are leaders. They step up to the plate and do what needs to be done for the staff and company to be safe, productive, and healthy. They defend their company the best they can with a secure environment and charted course of security measures, detect any threat to the company's assets, and quickly respond to the threat.

It's only common sense that the manager should be concerned with the cybersecurity of the business since lack of security can drastically affect every area of the business. A cyberattack can instantly shut down financial activity, communications, and operations of a business. Every manager should be concerned with *any* risk factor that has the potential to cripple or shut down the business. Every manager should understand their responsibility to initiate the appropriate action for such a risk.

Leaders Must Make Security Decisions

Cybersecurity is not a managerial task that is done once and forgotten. It is an ongoing task for managers to make decisions regarding the security of company data.

Managers know they cannot rely solely on technology to protect their organization. In addition to choosing software and technology that can help protect their network, managers must select and provide training for staff to understand security protocol and processes. (There is more on this later in this guide. But please understand the importance of the managerial task of training staff to understand security protocol and processes.)

In most cases, the security protocols can only be implemented or changed with the manager's approval. A manager who knows nothing about how to keep the company's information and networking system secure may not be capable of approving what they do not understand.

When a staff member approaches the manager with fundamental questions regarding computer and information security, leaders need to know the security principles to apply to the systems they want to secure from single computing devices to large network environments.

A manager who doesn't understand the basics of cybersecurity may have a problem conversing with the information technology department of their firm or external tech support to resolve cybersecurity issues when they arise.

Cybersecurity and the Mindset of the Leader

To protect their company, the leader must develop the mindset of a protective leader:

- Leaders understand that security is vital to the health of the company.
- Leaders know that prevention of an attack is the best cybersecurity but prevention requires constant awareness and effort.
- Leaders know that security from internal and external threats is a high-priority focus and a security solution must always be in place for both kinds of threats.
- Leaders are optimistic but realistic and know that every company is vulnerable to cybercrime.
- Leaders are aware that cyberattacks can be internal or external activity and the company must be secure from external and internal threats.
- Leaders know they must understand their company's vulnerabilities and be willing to address them.
- Leaders know that company security is dependent on constant vigilance and is not a one-time task. Solutions for cybersecurity is ongoing. Security health checks must be done at regular intervals.
- Leaders know that cybersecurity requires the leader to be involved and responsive to security issues.
- Leaders know that software alone cannot be relied upon for security.
- Leaders are willing to learn about and understand risk-mitigating measures to protect their company.

- Leaders who protect their company know they must invest the time and effort into becoming educated and trained as needed to help protect their company.

Business leaders must be willing to take their role in cybersecurity seriously. No, they do not serve as the IT team for the company, but they play an important leadership role when it comes to helping their company stay secure:

1. Leaders must be willing to become educated and trained for their part in the security of their company. They must be willing to set parameters and diligently guard the company data, intellectual property, finances, and sensitive information without fail.

2. When there is a threat to the company's security, leaders must understand the alerts and warnings provided by the security software and heed the

warnings. If the leader does not understand the alerts and warnings or does not heed them, the alerts and warnings are of none effect.

3. Once there is a warning or alert, the leader must respond according to the predetermined protocol to stop an attack or mitigate the threat.

4. The leader must be available and have the understanding to effectively perform their roles and guide the company through the recovery process after a threat or attack.

When the business leader knows their responsibility and role in the security of the company, they have taken the first step toward a more secure company.

4: Cybersecurity—An Underlying Issue

Whether it be competitors or other parties with malicious intent, numerous individuals and groups are looking for a way to gain access to your business network so they can use the information that is stored on your network for their intended purposes. For that reason, it's important to address the underlying issues of cybersecurity and ensure that protective measures are established to protect your company's digital data.

Understanding the underlying issues with cybersecurity will help you lay a firm foundation for further effective steps to protect your business. Once you and your staff understand the underlying issues and implement these three preventive principles, you will see an immediate improvement in cybersecurity in your organization. Understanding the underlying issues can also create momentum for launching your cybersecurity strategy details.

Three important principles w must be considered during daily business activities regarding information and data security:

1. Confidentiality
2. Integrity
3. Availability

In this chapter, the three basic principles that affect information security will be explored.

The Three Basic Principles That Affect Information Security

The security model of confidentiality, integrity, and availability was developed to help leaders understand the importance of cybersecurity and consider the most important factors that strengthen IT security and make it effective against cyberattacks.

Confidentiality

Taking measures with confidentiality helps prevent important sensitive information from reaching the wrong people while making sure it reaches the intended recipient that is allowed access to the information. For the enforcement of confidentiality, information that is confidential should be categorized as such, and only those who are authorized to view the confidential information should have access to it. Determining who should have access to confidential material stored online or sent back and forth via email and the level of confidentiality of the information should be predetermined.

To help determine confidentiality and security levels, ask the following questions: What would happen if a security breach compromised this information? How vulnerable would the company information be at each level of security? What departments or individuals would create vulnerability?

Security protocols must be properly implemented and enforced once the sensitivity of the information has been determined. People in the company who are authorized to receive and view information that is classified as sensitive or confidential information should receive training to ensure they are updated on the latest security measures and understand the security issues that could arise if confidential data was viewed by or sent to unintended recipients. Training should help authorized personnel understand the risk factors associated with the loss of information security, whether the loss is intentionally or unintentionally, and how they can best guard against the loss.

Authorized personnel should also understand how to create strong passwords and other password-related practices to guard against system vulnerabilities that could result in confidential information reaching the wrong person(s).

Authorized personnel should be required to participate in a two-factor authentication such as entering both a user ID and a password to access the information. In some instances, security tokens, biometric verification, soft tokens, or key fobs are good solutions for protecting confidential information.

The number of places from which highly-confidential information can be accessed and the number of times it can be accessed should be limited to all personnel even authorized personnel. In some instances, highly-sensitive information should be stored on devices that are not connected to the internet.

Integrity

Integrity is all about ensuring that data remains accurate consistently throughout its life cycle. It is critical that the company can trust that the data is accurate and original and has not been modified.

Data integrity security includes implementing security practices that help protect the data from being compromised by being modified or deleted by parties with malicious intent or without authorization to do so. Of course, the first security measure is to prevent unauthorized parties from gaining access to the data in the first place, but if this security measure fails, at least, the data should be secure so that it cannot be changed without authorization.

Data that may be appropriately modified should be specified as such and separated from data that should never be modified. As an example, account controls for the users should not be altered as the modifications could cause service disruption. On the other hand, user files are data that can be modified. Version control systems and traditional backups can be used for data that can be changed by authorized personnel only.

Security measures must be implemented that detect whether a change in data has been made. Methods used to verify the integrity of the data may include cryptographic checksums or simple checksums.

It is important to always backup all data and store it on another unlinked computer so that the original state of the data can be restored if data is maliciously or even accidentally modified or deleted.

Availability

Data must be available when required for people with authorization to view the information. This sounds like a simple aspect of security, but every factor that is used in the protection of data and in maintaining its integrity must work properly to ensure that all systems, authentication mechanisms, and access channels are available when needed. This requires that hardware must be rigorously maintained and that a highly-functioning operating system is designed and maintained by the organization. The design of the system determines what is available and what is not. The software used must be carefully chosen and configured to avoid conflicts, and all maintenance and upgrades must be completed on time.

Additionally, the IT person or department of the company must implement practices and safeguards that ensure availability of data without allowing data access to the unauthorized user.

Safeguards must be taken against the permanent loss of data or in the case of interruption of online connections. There should always be a backup of information that must be available. The backup data should be stored on an isolated computer in another geographical location to prevent permanent loss in the event of a cyberattack or even a natural disaster that could destroy office computers. In case of network intrusions or DoS (Denial of Service) attacks, enhanced security measures such as proxy servers and firewalls may be put in place for safeguarding data.

It is important to decide the various types of critical information that must be available at all times. Your server might need to handle the connection between multiple networks and routers to accommodate availability. Therefore, you should ensure that policies and practices are implemented that ensure that data availability issues are addressed promptly.

These three principles of security (CIA-Confidentiality, Integrity, and Availability) are an excellent benchmark model to evaluate the cybersecurity of your organization and take foundational steps to ensure that the business data is protected.

Data Theft

It is imperative that businesses keep their data confidential so that no unauthorized parties gain access to the data or modify it for malicious purposes. Availability of required data is also critical for every business. However, another underlying issue regarding cybersecurity is data theft.

Not to rehash the terrifying statistics mentioned in the previous chapters of this book regarding cyberattacks, but to emphasize the reality that, in recent years, there have been several incidents of data being stolen from major corporations and retailers, think about the Target breach of data in December 2013. With the Target breach, the personal and financial information of 70 million customers was stolen. This is just one example that data theft is a huge problem.

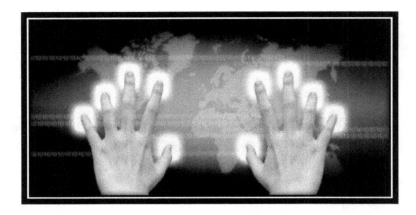

Identity theft occurs when hackers or thieves search for and steal a company's customers' specific personal information such as credit card numbers, date of birth, account numbers, personal identification numbers, social security numbers, and addresses. All this information can be used to steal the person's identity. Posing as the person whose information was stolen, the thieves can drain bank accounts, apply for, and receive new credit cards and credit accounts, purchase high-dollar items on credit that doesn't belong to them, and more. The thieves can also sell the stolen information to other criminals. Identity theft is a lucrative business for cybercriminals.

All companies are vulnerable to data theft. Data theft can happen internally or externally. But no matter how data theft happens, customers usually blame the company for not taking effective measures to protect their information. The data breach will negatively affect your business brand and reputation. Loyal customers may leave if they feel your company is not trustworthy. It is expensive to acquire customers the first time and even more expensive to woo them back after they leave. Additionally, with your focus, effort, and resources being utilized in gaining back lost customers, your competitors have the advantage of moving forward and may take a lead in the marketplace.

It's easy to understand that prevention is the best course of action for any company when it comes to data theft.

Non-Identity Data Theft

Businesses are hosts to various forms of confidential information, not just customer information, that thieves may steal for their malicious benefit. Confidential information may include proprietary product details or formulas that your competitors could use to develop for their own use and a competitive gain in the marketplace.

Confidential business information might provide details of business plans or strategies that could create problems for the company if it became public information.

You must implement and maintain strong and appropriate cybersecurity practices to protect confidential information even when it is not customer information. Note that this security is not limited to just computer files but should also include copiers and printers that are used by office staff that may not be authorized to access confidential files on the computers.

The Security Paradigm Has Shifted to Digital Information

As networks expand at such a pace that it has become difficult to keep pace with the expansion, and the attacks on said networks have become so frequent, ever-changing, and sophisticated, the security paradigm has shifted to safeguarding digital information and cybersecurity. Here are some factors that are changing the security paradigm:

- Security concerns have changed. They are no longer only limited to products but are also concerned with business objectives and procedures and tools for achieving such objectives.
- The number of threats is increasing daily, and this has given rise to workable solutions to maintain the effectiveness and efficiency of cyber security protocols. New and improved methods are utilized to prevent system breaches.

- Automated protocols and procedures to defend data against cyberattacks are critical because attacks occur at an exceptionally fast rate.

Security is not optimum if it is only enforced at the perimeter of the network. It must be implemented in every aspect of the network so that corrective methods can ensure the ultimate security framework for your business. Companies are constantly plagued with new viruses that are improved and more sophisticated. This requires cybersecurity controls installed in the business networks so that cyberattacks are rendered ineffective.

In this rapidly evolving environment where networks are increasing in size and capacity, the focus must be on managing and reducing the risks associated with cyber threats.

If the leader understands how the world of data protection and cybersecurity has changed and that data protection must be the focus of cybersecurity, your company can design and develop a strategy that encompasses all the important aspects of cybersecurity.

5: How Cybersecurity Works

Like it or not, the security of the company's data must be a high priority for every leader. For adequate protection against cyberattacks, your company must have a coordinated strategy in place. The strategy should involve people, processes, and controls, all working together for the goal of security.

Your IT department will handle the technical aspects of cybersecurity, but there must be a strategy and processes in place that includes the business leader and the staff. The leader must be ready to do their part to ensure that critical information is protected with the best cybersecurity the company can provide.

In this chapter, you will learn how cybersecurity works and what you can do to protect the data and other assets of your business. Let's start with the Ten Dimensions of Cybersecurity.

The Ten Dimensions of Cybersecurity

The ten dimensions of cybersecurity is a framework that you can use for managing cybersecurity performance. It is a roadmap, of sorts, that can help you focus on safeguarding crucial data from critical threats.

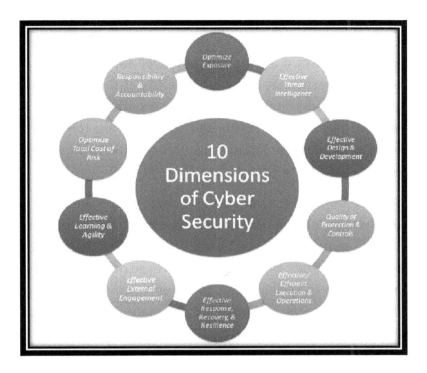

The graphic above summarizes the ten dimensions that are discussed in the next ten chapters of this guide. If you understand these ten dimensions, you will understand how cybersecurity works and what you can do to ensure good cybersecurity practices in your organization.

In the realm of cybersecurity, people interact with a system. Through those interactions, certain events or instances may arise that may have a positive or negative effect on your business.

The people who interact with the system may be a part of the business, or they may be external parties. They could be individuals or an organization other than your organization, interacting with a device, computer, or software through which an event may or may not arise. If the people are legitimate users that have authority to access data, all is well. If they are not authorized users but are third-party users with malicious intent to acquire sensitive information or to sabotage the information, there is a problem.

The systems these people interact with could be a technology, information, process, or a combination of these things, along with the physical facilities that enable the people to interact with the systems. These people must also have access to certain types of support-providing facilities that are physical in nature to facilitate the interaction process.

Events, as mentioned previously, are the resulting instances or occurrences that might have a positive or a negative impact on the daily activities of a business.

While it's important to focus on minimizing the threats and risks associated with information sharing through good cybersecurity practices, it is also important to strengthen the security measures that are already in place for the business. That is why it is critical for the proper operation of any business to ensure that its cybersecurity protocols are effective.

Before delving into the ten dimensions, three important factors should be considered when employing the cybersecurity practices within your organization:

1. The dimensions that will be discussed in detail later must be implemented and followed across cross-functional teams and organizations.
2. When you understand the different functions, you will identify many similarities between them. That is why they are not mentioned as separate dimensions, but rather as functions that are distributed among the existing ten dimensions.
3. The performance of each dimension is dependent upon the nature of each organization, along with the objectives that drive the business. Therefore, one performance factor cannot be compared with any other organization, as every organization's dimensions may vary greatly.

In the next ten chapters of this guide, you will learn the ten dimensions of cybersecurity. The chapters are intentionally short, so you can absorb the details of each dimension, answer the questions specifically for your organization, and think about how you can implement what you have learned in your business. Take notes as you go and get the most out of each chapter.

6: Dimension One—Exposure Optimization

The first dimension of cybersecurity is the *exposure optimization*. This is where business leaders and executives join the journey of information management. The business leader must monitor the positive and negative interaction between systems and actors, and evaluate the impact on the organization and its data from those interactions. They must also handle breaches and tackle cyberattacks that pose an immense threat to the business.

Again, you have users and systems that interact with one another, and their interaction leads to events. Optimizing exposure is the starting point for the performance of all cybersecurity measures in place within your business. You must understand and optimize the exposure of information and systems to breaches, attacks, or violations. Exposure mediates between actors and systems. Exposure means that the users have access to the system and all systems are visible. Hence, the systems may be potentially vulnerable. Optimization means balancing tradeoffs, i.e., the negative interactions (in which a system's breach occurred) and positive interactions (in which only the authorized party gained access to the system).

It is imperative that all business managers realize that cybersecurity cannot be taken lightly. The manager must understand when and where to expose parties to critical information and how to monitor the number of people within the organization that can view specific pieces of information. Limiting and specifying the number of authorized viewers can help prevent impromptu and unintentional cyberthreats such as mistakenly viewing confidential information. It also allows the manager to take preventive actions as necessary. Optimizing exposure of parties that have authorized access helps reduce cyberthreats, risks, and attacks, and helps the business to function more efficiently.

Exposure helps in mediating information between the people and the systems used to gain access to any form of data. If a person has exposure to a piece of information, that means that data is accessible and visible through the system used to obtain it. This can make the system vulnerable to external threats.

Limiting the number of people who have access to the data can help balance the negative impacts by limiting exposure of the data while maximizing the positive impacts through enhancing exposure to the relevant, authorized users.

Cyber performance based on this dimension optimizes all efforts toward improving management of the potential people that are exposed to the data. Therefore, the aim of any leader should be to converse with the IT departments and cybersecurity professionals and work with them on the objective of identifying the tradeoffs of following this framework and determining which options should be traded off, and which should be implemented. This dimension is based upon two components: intelligence and execution.

The Intelligence Component

The intelligence component involves observing the level of cybersecurity protection your business currently possesses and then evaluating this current standard. Then you must decide where your current cybersecurity efforts stand, compare this against the changing environment, and decide the desired protection level to obtain maximum security against malicious cyber activity. This process is known as performing a *gap analysis.*

Along with the gap analysis, the intelligence component must also answer certain key questions that will help you obtain a clear picture of where your cybersecurity level currently stands. These questions will help you determine whether there are any flaws in your cybersecurity policies and, if there are, what can be done to close the gaps:

- What information is exposed?
- What information is not exposed?
- What information should be exposed?
- What information should not be exposed?
- Are we currently meeting the standard for what should be exposed?
- Are we currently exposing information that should not be exposed? What should we do about it?
- What action plan and strategies can help us attain the maximum level of cybersecurity?

The questions above will give you the appropriate guidelines regarding the proper procedure for communicating with the relevant people about their responsibilities for protecting critical information. This entails involving the people who are part of the interaction process and clearly communicating about the information that should be kept confidential.

The Execution Component

Once you have identified where the gaps lie in your cybersecurity, you must devise a strategy to overcome the gaps and to effectively execute your security. Executing this framework entails implementing the decisions you made regarding the protection of information.

Execution includes implementing some of the common security practices and general policies related to cybersecurity such as access, control, system configurations, remediation, privileges, vulnerability detection, and related policies. However, it's important to note that the execution component is not only the technical aspects of cybersecurity but also involves the Human Resources department to create policies that regulate information disclosures and the penalties associated with the disclosure of information. The HR department will help define privacy, proprietary, and confidentiality of information penalties.

Clear definitions help you determine what information is critical to run the business and what must be kept confidential; what can be disclosed and what must never be disclosed because the confidentiality of such information is critical to the health and profitability of the company.

Intelligence and execution should work in conformity without making the policies too strict or too lax, resulting in a framework that is not too rigid or too loose.

Exposure optimization is a huge responsibility and does not solely depend upon the performance of a single business unit. Every department must actively participate in deciding which data is important enough to receive confidentiality status. The implementation of both these components depends on all departments working in unison. It is the responsibility of each department to communicate regarding confidential data to avoid unnecessary confusion and accidental viewing of private information.

Additionally, all employees must be responsible for protecting data from malicious attacks. This means all managers and leaders need to be aware of the data already accessible by employees and setting security levels for the data.

Given an ideal cyberworld, there would be a single composite measure of exposure composed of two metrics, i.e., the attack surface metric and exposure surface metric. The attack surface metric measures the area of any cyber interface or network that was targeted during an attack, while the exposure surface metric measures the extent of information that is available for access by the relevant, authorized parties. The larger the exposure surface, the greater the chance of successful cyberattacks, as threat agents have more opportunities of identifying the vulnerabilities within the system.

These metrics are mentioned to stress the importance of limiting the exposure surface. The larger the exposure surface is, the greater the potential of increased cyberthreats. The larger the exposure surface, the easier it becomes for cybercriminals to find loopholes in the system through which they can enter and destroy the hard drive or access confidential data. There can even be specified regions within the exposed surface that are more vulnerable than others.

Consider the following questions when you need to determine how well your cybersecurity practices are working in the dimension of optimized exposure. Talk with your IT manager to get the answers. They will assist you in making the entire system more secure.

- How well are we currently performing in preventing our information systems exposure?
- How much do we know about the exposure of information within the system and the cyberthreats faced by the organization?
- Are we aware of any blind spots in the system? If we are, then what are we doing to offset the effects and bridge the gaps emerging within the system?
- Have we made any discoveries in the significant exposure areas? Are we addressing the areas and increasing security?
- How well have we fared in executing the decisions we have made so far?

- What is the evidence of our decisions being successful? Have we made the right tradeoffs for the system and our business?
- What is our capability for handling and maintaining tabs on the exposure of information?
- Are we optimizing our capability of information exposure? Is our performance getting better?
- Are we stuck at a specified position? If yes, then is our performance in information exposure declining? What should be done to improve performance?

Each of these questions should have their own performance metrics so that it becomes easier to evaluate the current standing regarding cybersecurity effectiveness and in identifying the various exposure points in the system that need improvement. Again, the metrics will differ from one organization to the next.

7: Dimension Two—Threat Intelligence and Its Effectiveness

The second dimension involves understanding the various threat agents that pose a threat to your organization and the different measures you can take to protect your organization. People, their interactions with different systems, and the events resulting from such interactions, as well as the level of access given to certain people who use the system, has already been introduced.

Threat agents have a direct impact on the exposure of any information. When you want to mediate between the people and the systems through which they can access sensitive information, threat intelligence plays a role in detecting changes.

To determine the factors that threaten your business and which can be used to your benefit, consider your answers to the following questions:

- What might be a threat to our information?

- Who might want to gain access to our information?
- In what context or setting do we consider an identified party a potential threat?
- What are the potential methods through which the threat agents might target the company?
- What are the capabilities of the identified threat agents?
- What might be of interest to these threat agents?
- How can these threat agents benefit from the information we possess?
- How can information leakage to the threat agents affect us negatively?

The effectiveness of security is an important dimension. Online fraud attempts that are targeted toward specific businesses are increasing at an alarming rate.

Intelligent threat awareness includes two types of activities. Generic threat activities consist of offline activities and attempts at gaining access to critical information. It also includes real-time threats that are more specific in nature and are targeted toward particular exposure gaps. Developing intelligence regarding the different people or parties that might want to harm your business by cyberattacks to gain access to information or to overload your server can help you prepare for such attempts. As well as developing intelligence regarding those who might want to attack, there should also be focused consideration of the various types of tools that could be used to cause harm to the business.

Keep in mind that not all threat agents will be of malicious intent. Human error can also result in security breaches. Such breaches make the business more vulnerable to external attacks.

Deciding whether to employ cybersecurity tactics and strategies can be a difficult decision for small and new businesses due to expense concerns. They may feel they do not have the resources to take effective measures for implementing advanced cybersecurity protocols within their organization. However, as established earlier in this text, *all* businesses are targeted for cyberattacks and small, and new businesses are no exception. It is a necessity for all businesses, large and small, to focus part of their business strategy and resources on protecting confidential data.

If the business doesn't have a department large enough to oversee the cybersecurity matters, it should try to outsource the responsibility to cybersecurity service providers, but never ignore the cybersecurity issue.

If you want to measure your performance in this dimension, you should study the level of effectiveness. Focus on how well the actions have been taken, if actions were implemented correctly, and whether you and your organization are doing the correct things required for effective cybersecurity. You can't necessarily pay attention to every threat, but pay close attention to the most important threat agents and try to find out the details about them.

8: Dimension Three—Cyber Interface— Designing and Developing Effectively

The third dimension is focused on the design and development of a cybersecurity interface, along with the design and development of the organization. The design of the cybersecurity interface must take into consideration the size of the organization and the amount of data that is stored on its servers. A framework must be created that helps guide the organization's cybersecurity protocols, thereby protecting the organization from external risk factors. The design must be done carefully after analyzing the various threats faced by the organization, thereby giving clear direction to the cybersecurity professionals regarding the level of security that must be implemented.

Once the design has been created, then comes the process of development. Development includes realizing what the design is and analyzing it to ensure that there are no gaps in the entire process. Once the gaps have been determined, the design should be redefined and adjustments made accordingly.

Design and development dimension consists of the creation of systems with which people interact to gain access to important or confidential information. It provides a comprehensive concept through which the architecture of the system is created, and the foundation is laid for preparing the systems. This architecture explains in detail how the system is going to work and how it will generate output that will lead to the creation of events. The events would occur in response to the interaction of a person with the system.

This dimension includes all the design and development activities that are part of a business. Following are the components that make it a comprehensive dimension, inclusive of all design and development activities that might be undertaken in an organization:

- The design and development of hardware
- The design and development of software
- The architecture of the organization
- The design and development of the business process
- The architecture of data and information
- The design and development of the organization

- Contract design
- Relationship with partners: distribution, supply chain, and outsourced partners
- Incentive systems
- Internal and external governance factors

To ensure optimal performance of your cybersecurity strategy, this dimension is considered extremely important. By focusing on these key aspects, improvements to cybersecurity could be made systematically, thereby maximizing the received benefits.

Most companies continually neglect this important dimension and, therefore, suffer the consequences in the form of recurring malfunctions in the systems. It is only at this stage that the quality of the entire cybersecurity system could be enhanced and improved instead of postponing it and allowing threats that might exploit your system's weaknesses, leading to security breaches and malicious attacks.

Neglecting this dimension can lead to a serious negative situation for most businesses, where the cybersecurity is not effective in creating the barriers needed for protecting critical data and resulting in financial loss.

To manage the performance in this dimension, you must pay close attention to the effectiveness of your decisions. Consider your answers to the following questions to help determine where you stand:

- Have the right decisions been made regarding the design and development of our business?
- Is the design of our cybersecurity effecting in thwarting threats?
- How has the design affected the performance of our business?
- Is the development of our prepared design effective in protecting and securing confidential data?

The above questions can help you focus on the design of the various components and make them stronger. But how can you determine whether these designs are effective and will meet your business and cybersecurity objectives? You can discuss the various factors that are important for creating the designs. Once you have identified the factors, think of the different way each design interacts with a factor. These factors include the following:

- Technology
- Organization structures
- Business processes
- Policies and procedures
- The systems used to create the designs

Keep in mind that these dimensions apply to large and small organizations, new and established businesses, and at every stage of the business. The business managers should learn as much as they can to lead their staff in cybersecurity issues, but they may also feel comfortable hiring the services of a professional.

9: Dimension Four— Protection and Control Quality of Cybersecurity

The quality of the controls you use for the protection of private and confidential data will prevent cyberthreats from actively affecting the level of your exposed information. The better these security controls, the higher the security of your data, which can be made even more effective by limiting the exposure of information to unauthorized users.

Sometimes, potential threats can be eliminated entirely by modifying the systems toward providing enhanced security. This dimension also considers the different designs of the systems so that the protection provided considers all those factors. Certain threats may be eliminated entirely, but cyber systems will always face threats in one form or another.

These protection controls may also be the way people interact. They can also be implemented in systems in such a way that they immediately alert the responsible person whenever a threat is detected. Security and privacy awareness programs may serve as a good example of this. They help educate the organization's employees about the various cyberthreats and how to overcome them, which protocols to follow in case of a breach, and how to prevent the transfer of information to malicious parties. Ensuring that you are prepared for even the most unexpected breach can ensure that your data remains safe.

This dimension includes bringing in the specialists to do the work. For some organizations, this means hiring professionals. For other organizations, it means working with the IT department. The specialized teams will focus on implementing cybersecurity while ensuring all the other possibilities that you might overlook are addressed. Following are some of the areas that the professional teams are responsible for:

- Access Control
- Identity Management Intrusion Detection and Prevention
- Malware Detection and Removal
- Ex-filtration Controls and much more

These factors are quite effective in lowering risks, dealing with cyberthreats, and in designing strategies by using different programs like firewalls and password-protected documents.

For business managers, it is important to measure this dimension to determine how well the company is performing regarding the quality of the cybersecurity strategies used. Therefore, experts recommend measuring the performance of this dimension based on quality. Your IT professionals will know what quality of protection entails; however, it is your duty to ensure that your IT managers focus on the quality of service as well. This has a significant impact on network design and makes the workings of various networks easier to manage.

How do you determine whether the cybersecurity protocols that have been implemented meet the standards of quality? To answer this question, you must get the answers to the following questions:

- How effective is our current cybersecurity performance?
- Have the implemented controls thwarted any threats that might pose a danger to the company's profitability?
- Does our cybersecurity framework conform to the quality specifications?
- Do the controls work as intended? Are there unintended consequences that were not anticipated?
- What is the level of deficiencies being faced currently? What can we do to improve the quality of the current cybersecurity protocols?
- Are our current cybersecurity efforts meeting our security needs of safeguarding critical information and limiting access to unauthorized users?

Business leaders must understand the intended purpose of implementing a system and its protocols. Only after you know this should you decide on metrics to judge the quality of your cybersecurity practices. Also, determine what would be considered satisfactory performance according to your business standards, identify where the system deficiencies lie, then develop a method to analyze the quality and performance of your company's cybersecurity strategy.

This should be done for every individual process and control used for the protection of important data and then, if possible, for the collection of protection controls. Quality of the controls used for protection, as well as the resulting level of protection, must be measured directly. This will give you a better understanding of your cybersecurity controls.

You can accomplish this through time series analysis to check the total number of attempts to breach your security in comparison to the number of attempts that were successful in gaining access to your data. Time series analysis is an analysis of the past data that is carried out with the assumption that every event or series of events has a trend or seasonal variation. It helps in analyzing past hacking attempts, both successful and unsuccessful, thereby providing an idea of future trends. To some extent, this can help you devise strategies to overcome and eliminate future hacking attempts.

One of the questions that you were previously asked to consider was whether the controls are working as intended and, if not, what are the consequences that were previously unseen. This is a serious issue that must be addressed quickly so that the effects of any mistakes in data security can be curtailed. This issue is most often seen in organizations that have strict protocols without consideration for any room for improvement. For such companies, it is even more important to question the way things are run and challenge the assumptions with the objective of improving the cybersecurity operations.

Evaluate how well the controls have been implemented and whether they have been implemented to the right specifications. Neglecting this can result in significant cost and loss to your business, particularly if a malicious party succeeds in breaching your cybersecurity.

An example of how you can ensure the effectiveness of your data protection controls is to implement a system in which all employees must provide two forms of identification to gain access to the data. With this system, you can check how well your security protocols are faring against real-time implemented procedures and check for any discrepancies in the records.

If your security protocols only allow authorized personnel to gain access to the information, your protection controls are effectively working as intended. However, if an employee who does not possess proper authorization is able to gain access, you have a problem.

Also, check whether the two identification forms, as specified in the system, appear whenever an employee tries to access the information. If the employee can gain access without having to input information in the identification forms, then the system should report an error. Ask your staff to report any incident when they gained access to confidential information without filling in the identification forms.

You should also try to determine how quickly and promptly the number of invalid identifications are detected and how they are tackled. Along with this, also consider the following questions:

- How often does the database malfunction?
- How often are internal threats detected?
- How often is the database out of sync with the number of authorized personnel?
- How often does the database and cybersecurity system detect incorrectly and provide access to unauthorized personnel?
- Has your cybersecurity recently updated?
- How is your cybersecurity protection control performing compared to six weeks ago?
- To what extent has the number of potential cyberattacks and threats decreased?

Thoroughly analyzing your company's current situation can enable you to develop action plans that are effective in maintaining the quality of the protection and control of your cybersecurity.

Now, the question that you must ask is how you are going to measure the quality of the system that protects your data from cyberattacks. The answer lies in the methods and modes of interactions. According to Jens Groossklags, who made use of Game Theory to come up with three different games, here are three methods by which the quality of a system and its efficacy and effectiveness can be gained:

- Total Effort—When the controls mutually support one another, and the party that interacts with the system is a group of people instead of an individual, then total effort can be measured, as the quality of protection is proportional to the sum of all quality controls.
- Weakest Link—It has often been said that a team is only as good as its weakest link. The same can be said about the quality of cybersecurity protocols. In this case, the quality of your data protection should be proportional to the weakest control—the control that has the lowest quality. Failure of such controls can result in a breach by an unknown third party.
- Best Shot—This metric is the exact opposite of the Weakest Link. It means that quality is proportional to the best control that provides the highest quality to the system. When controls are operating in a series, the optimal level of protection provided by one control helps to thwart breach attempts made by malicious parties.

Protection and control quality are important dimensions in the cybersecurity picture.

10: Dimension Five—Execution and Operations

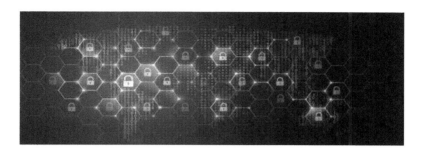

The fifth dimension includes the operations and their executions, how effective they are, and how efficient they can be. It has a similar relationship with the other dimensions as the quality controls dimension. Along with this, the fifth dimension also encompasses the design and development of the systems so they can be exposed to relevant parties.

Execution and operation has a relationship with the other dimension of quality of protection and control and is mutually supportive. The execution and operation dimension helps to implement the plans that have been created during the protection and controls dimension. This is the engine that actually gets the work done in cybersecurity.

Through this dimension, businesses can create another path through which people can interact with the systems. This dimension consists of implementing the action plans for cybersecurity and then effectively monitoring those actions.

This dimension includes logging, reporting, training, configuring, patching, updating, and all other related functions, undertaking the plans that have been devised previously and then implementing them. Development operations, commonly referred to in the software industry as Dev Ops, is a concept developed by the software industry.

Paying close attention to your cybersecurity decisions is important. The different operations that must be implemented to ensure your data stays protected are part of this dimension. In fact, this is one of the most significant dimensions because of the impact on overall security. If implemented correctly, this dimension can boost the security level of your business and optimize it to its complete potential.

Operational errors can result in huge business losses and create further cybersecurity problems. It's important to ensure that your system is free of all defects. Improper implementation can lead to dire consequences. The case of Windows Azure is a good example. The outage of Windows Azure led to an operational error that resulted in the expiration of SSL certificates. This outage resulted in a significant financial loss for Microsoft. Apart from the costs associated with the response and recovery of the data, Microsoft had to provide millions of dollars of compensation to their customers. Most companies cannot endure such a loss.

How can you view the execution of the decisions you have made regarding the operations of the business? The entire system of operation must be considered as a whole and measured by considering it as a performance dimension and looking at the effectiveness of its results.

This dimension needs to be effective to ensure that the right things are implemented. Instead of doing a little of everything, it is best to focus on the high-priority items and implement those. Identifying the most important aspects of cybersecurity and deciding what should be made a priority is a challenging task. The demands of cybersecurity change constantly. Even the introduction of new software can create the need to completely revamp the cybersecurity strategy. Again, the circumstances that affect cybersecurity may be internal or external. It is important to focus on every aspect that could have a positive or negative impact on your cybersecurity. However, the effectiveness of the factors that have been chosen for implementation is also very important. Selecting and implementing the right controls is just one part of executing operations. What matters, even more, is making sure the controls are correctly and efficiently implemented.

The result of your performance is dependent on how well and how fast a decision was executed with regards to the cybersecurity protocols. These performances mostly depend upon fast cycle time, the speed with which they are delivered, peak volume capacity, and throughput. All leaders must ensure that the plans are in conjunction with the corporate goals and objectives and that the cybersecurity analyst implements them as designed and discussed in the data security strategy for the business.

Leaders have the responsibility for overseeing that all the operations are performing as intended, and if not, retracing the steps from the beginning and determining the mistake. This should be done with the intention of improving the overall cybersecurity system. Though it may seem easier to ignore the performance and not admit that mistakes were made, admitting your mistake can help eliminate the factors that resulted in the ineffective performance of the security network and ensuring that all gaps are addressed.

The quality of the protocols and decisions implemented also affect the performance level of your security protocols. As with everything else in your business, cybersecurity must also have objectives, and the objectives must be determined and specified before the execution of operations because they will guide the decision-making process.

The method by which you can determine the performance level of your business must be considered by asking the following question: How do we bring the things we designed to reality? This question will help you decide how to make your desired results a reality. It is imperative that you decide the "how," and the "how" will lead you to the "why."

The how consists of the action plan that ensures your objectives are met. The why considers all your decisions and outlines your goals and objectives that help create a plan of action. However, this should not be taken in the context of solely this dimension. It should encompass all dimensions, thereby enabling you to see a clear picture of the entire system.

All the elements explained thus far, and the ones that will be explained in the following dimensions operate in conjunction with one another. Only by ensuring that all these factors complement one another and work harmoniously can ensure that your computer systems and networks are optimally secured. Each dimension must be connected to the other with the common task of tight security against cyberthreats and cyberattacks. This is a good reason for you to work well with your IT department or team so everyone is on the same page.

Additionally, you must be open to changes in the system because change is inevitable. In fact, the business manager should implement changes when they see the changes can benefit the business in some way.

To support cybersecurity operations, this dimension includes data logging, data sensing, and data reporting—all which help to implement cybersecurity strategy. You should understand how focusing on the proper execution of the cybersecurity operations can help your business remain protected from external threats and can help you formulate effective action plans that achieve your intended results.

11: Dimension Six—Timely Response and Recovery

Have you ever been a position when you felt your laptop looked like the one in the picture above? If so, you know that recovery from a malicious attack must be quick and effective. Otherwise, business as you know it can come to a screeching halt.

You read about the fifth dimension and how it concerns responding to cyberthreats promptly and recovering from any damages quickly. As a business manager, you must be proactive and respond quickly to actions from your competition to sabotage your business through cyberattacks of any kind. This requires constant effort and a drive for optimum security always. However, instances may arise when cyberattacks are successful, and your competitors gain an advantage. What do you do then? You come up with a strategy that helps you regain the position you lost.

For a business to be responsive to competitors or to an external environment, it must take prompt actions and engage in war against the competition. But what determines whether it's the right time to respond to the competition or to help the business recover from the competitor's attacks? The answer to that question is dependent on the circumstances that arise as a result of the interactions between systems and people.

Just as it is important for businesses to promptly respond to competitor attempts to take over the market share, it is just as important for the cybersecurity of a business to respond to external and internal threats. The incidents that occur because of people interacting with systems could vary from minor incidents due to human error to high-priority security breaches that compromise confidential data. The leader should be informed about each scenario.

The sixth dimension of timely response and recovery is closely linked to executions and operations. The effectiveness of executed operations will determine how quickly you can respond to threats and cyberattacks. The timely response and recovery dimension covers the following processes:

- Incidence response
- Business and legal response
- Digital forensics
- Recovery of lost data
- Regulation of data

You may also include factors that promote resilience, meaning factors that allow the system to continue to operate even in the face of cyberattacks. It is important for the leader to discuss and address resilience factors with the IT department and security staff.

One of the significant issues that a company faces when there is cyberattack on their database or network is the time it takes to recover from the attack. Response time will vary and depends on how quickly you become aware of the attack. The longer the response time, the more damage the company may suffer, including loss of data. If the response time is effective or delayed, the system infiltrators have the chance to grab as much data as possible in a very short amount of time.

Leaders should never make the mistake of covering up an incident to avoid "looking bad on their watch" or out of fear of not knowing how to handle the situation. Failing to respond can cause tremendous damage and even lead to multiple lawsuits and other legal problems.

The focus on response and recovery should be how effective it is but, also, how efficiently and quickly the matter was handled. Ineffective response time is often the cause of severe data loss.

Whether threats are averted or carried out, the leader must be on top of the situation and work with the IT and security departments for recovery.

Ineffective response times are often the cause of severe data loss. The gaps must be identified and

All managers, staff, and legal support should be made aware of incidents that may drastically affect the business or require significant security changes. It is always best to be prepared for the worst-case scenario and hope for the best.

12: Dimension Seven—External Environment—Understanding the Risk Factors

The external environment dimension helps guide the cybersecurity and setting requirements and constraints for its operational procedures to ascertain that the protocols are exceptionally adept at protecting important data. Understanding the external environment and who may be trying to target your business gives you a better idea of what is best for securing your company from attacks. It is important to understand who might have enough of a stake in the organization's demise to launch a severe cyberattack. You should also know the external drivers that help strengthen your cybersecurity. These drivers include cybersecurity service providers, internet service providers, DNS service providers, certificate authorities, registrars, and others.

Leaders must make sure their cybersecurity team consists of qualified, capable, trustworthy people who have the expertise and knowledge to implement and execute cybersecurity actions that are directed toward the ultimate attainment of the company's objectives. Again, the company's cybersecurity objectives should align with the company's overall objectives.

A good manager knows the external environment of the business, in general, and when it comes to cybersecurity. The players who are part of the cybersecurity team, either directly or indirectly, must be considered when you determine that changes need to be made for remaining ahead of the competitor's external threat agents. Change is important. Change may come through change drivers or by creating change agents such as technological advancements or improvements in the process. Becoming a change driver can be difficult, but it can be accomplished by considering the external forces that are part of the environment and regarding how their actions or strategies can impact the organization.

All of this must be taken in the context of cybersecurity as you focus and point out how security protocols can affect the protection levels of your business. Managing technological relationships is only part of the dimension. You must also focus on how these relationships can pose a threat to your business or benefit your business. You must also consider whether any of these key players have any influence on your organization directly or indirectly and ensure that any actions taken by them cannot harm your business.

The leader must ensure that the procedures and protocols installed are in line with industry standards. It is imperative for leaders to think of the various digital platforms that can be used as the basis of attack by any malicious party in the external environment.

Business managers must also consider the changing trends and how they can impact the company and affect other risk drivers. With the advancement of technology, the risk drivers become more sophisticated almost daily. New software is constantly introduced, which completely transforms the manner which previous cybersecurity protocols worked. Leaders must be prepared for the entire security paradigm to change with the introduction of new programs.

By understanding the different methods through which other organizations can put you at risk, or through which actions your organization could suffer, you can take corrective and preventive actions without the consequences of an actual attack.

13: Dimension Eight—Agility and Learning— Innovating Cybersecurity

Every successful organization realizes it must change with the times or get left behind. For cybersecurity, it is crucial that the leader is open to change and is proactive rather than reactive.

Dimension eight includes the implementation of cybersecurity and then restructuring and re-engineering it until it becomes an innovated, new infrastructure. Organizations must learn from their past actions, positive and negative, and constantly improve their systems. Remaining agile in the face of competitors can help sustain your business over the long term.

There must always be metrics that are used to measure the performance level of each dimension. In this dimension, it is also important to analyze the performance of the *entire* system that is implemented for the protection of the company's data. Even though each individual dimension calls for specific metrics, the whole is not always equal to the sum of its parts. You can't get a clear picture of the loopholes that are present in your cybersecurity system until you have assessed how well the entire system works and considered the effectiveness of each dimension and how well they are interrelated.

Your complete portfolio of cybersecurity protocols must be reviewed to study the system and figure out which areas need improvement, and which are performing better than the rest, which needs to be taken out of the system or revamped to include additional areas of security.

You can identify the relevant areas that require excessive improvement and those which can be left untouched only after you study and analyze the entire structure of your cybersecurity system. This also tells you whether the critical information of your organization is being kept safe by protocols, how effective the provided protection is, and whether any other changes can be made to ensure that no threat is able to override your data's security.

You can also look at the areas that pose no current threat to your company and consider the possibilities should those areas become a threat in the future. Keep in mind that there is no such thing as overprotection when it comes to cybersecurity! You should consider all worst-case scenarios.

Part of the learning dimension is taking incremental steps of improvement that lead to innovative methods of implementing cybersecurity. Think about creating new possibilities for your future business security. Imagine if a program was launched that completely revamped the way businesses implement cybersecurity. Take big leaps by creating protocols that leave behind the old capabilities and give birth to new capabilities.

Leaders must go back to the initiating point of cybersecurity and look at how it is implemented currently, then challenge all assumptions and create cybersecurity protocols again. In doing so, you may come up with protocols that strengthen your security. If you are biased about your security protocols and insist on remaining with them, you will miss opportunities for improvement.

To find out if this dimension can be measured and how it can be measured, you must be able to measure the time it takes to innovate the entire process of implementing and executing cybersecurity. You must consider how much time it took to come up with the ideas and how long it took for those ideas to be accepted by your organization.

Your security framework must be based on changes, and these changes must be different from what is widely accepted within your industry. If your security only consists of what is already implemented by everyone in the industry, your company would be vulnerable to attacks from malicious parties. If you have a few innovative implementations, you reduce risk.

Learning encompasses more than making mistakes and ensuring that they don't reoccur. Learning also includes trial and error activities that lead to breakthroughs in the protective framework of your cybersecurity protocols. You must be able to react to environmental changes quickly and efficiently, meaning you must find solutions for various situations.

The business leader must be prepared for sudden changes. Your team is counting on your leadership during times of change. Reconfigure your resources, structure them according to the changing times, and ensure that you have implemented security protocols that are directed toward the attainment of maximum cybersecurity. You must continually learn and adapt and so must your staff.

Learn effectively, so you don't repeat mistakes. Change according to the requirements of your business. Use your past mistakes as a stepping stone toward running a secure business.

Do not ignore this dimension. It is imperative as it can be the driver of change within the cybersecurity framework of your organization.

14: Dimension Nine—Optimizing the Costs Associated with Risks

Dimension nine includes all the procedures and processes that help in the assessment and management of cybersecurity, particularly regarding resources, liabilities, risk mitigation, and forming a balance between the cyber risks faced by an organization and its strengths.

This dimension is concerned with the costs that are associated with cybersecurity, the implementation, failure to comply with the procedures, and ineffective provision of security to the entire framework.

It is important to make a list of all the risks that might affect your business and could occur because of activity or incidents related to cybersecurity. Your defenses can only be strong if you have a correct estimation of your risks and risk factors. All risk factors must be considered financially, and their impact on the financial standing and performance of the company should be considered.

Take account of all the costs that are related to your cybersecurity protocols and determine which costs must be considered under this dimension. This dimension takes some elements of Total Quality Management, links them with cybersecurity, and then considers the intended and unintended consequences that could affect the costs in any matter. This effect can be either an increase or decrease in cybersecurity costs. The costs that are a result of breaches and incident must also be taken into account so that a clear picture can be created of the total amount of losses you would face if such incidents occurred.

This dimension does not demand that you be accurate with the costs, rather it is aimed at giving business managers and executives an idea of the costs so they can make informed decisions regarding the implementation of cybersecurity. Once you understand the overall costs, you can attribute specific amounts toward specific elements. This enables you to identify the area with the highest costs and make decisions according to budget approval.

The measures of such costs must be done every quarter. Over a few quarters, you will recognize that a pattern emerges. The exception is if there is a huge cybersecurity breach that creates extensive damage and causes costs to surge. Though this is, hopefully, rare, do not disregard such incidents. Consider the resulting tangible and intangible losses of an extensive breach. Data analysis can help you detect the trend of such incidents and help you uncover a systematic pattern that may determine what area is likely to be hit by external threat agents.

As a leader, it is not wise to ignore this dimension. Understanding the risks can help you with various decisions that are your responsibility.

15: Dimension Ten— Responsibility and Accountability

Dimension ten, the top management's responsibility and accountability to stakeholders, ties all the other dimensions together. All business departments, no matter how large or small, must work together toward clear company objectives. This is true for the objective of strong cybersecurity for the company. When every department understands the importance of cybersecurity, agrees on the various protocols that must be implemented, and is willing to take responsibility for their role in the protection of critical data, implementing cybersecurity is not difficult.

This dimension includes all the previous directives and takes them from the perspective of the decision makers. The decision makers are the one key factor in linking all the dimensions together for creating a sustainable cybersecurity framework. However, all the decisions cannot be made by the executives; stakeholders may be included in the decision-making process indirectly through their feedback.

When the ownership of everything that goes on in an organization is taken by the stakeholders, it is easy to implement change and ensure that correct cybersecurity measures are in place. Every decision maker is accountable for his or her actions, and the responsibility of overseeing the implementation of decisions sits on the shoulders of the top management.

Each must take some responsibility for overseeing the implementation of cybersecurity protocols and procedures. They must participate proactively in developing competence and executing the tasks required for the proper implementation of cybersecurity. Taking ownership entails focusing on what needs to be done and initiating tasks that are not necessarily part of the job description.

Business managers should ask who is responsible for what and to what extent when it comes to cybersecurity. The major problem that is faced by most businesses is that, most of the time, business managers do not take their responsibility as leaders when it comes to cybersecurity.

Accountability is specifying those few individuals who are held responsible if a cybersecurity decision goes wrong and results in negative consequences for the company. This also tests the level of commitment of each person to an organization. Therefore, it becomes extremely important to determine which people must be considered at-fault when a decision backfires on the company.

Usually, as the decision-making power rests in the hands of the top executives and managers, the accountability for such decisions also rests with them. The cybersecurity team and certain employees who were part of a team that made decisions may also shoulder some of the responsibility for decisions.

This dimension allows business managers and executives to create an environment of trust between them and their stakeholders. It helps in creating strong relationships that result in better decisions.

Responsibility and accountability must be measured broadly. Business managers can achieve this by looking at the way the people within your organization take charge of a situation. There are clues present if you observe and notice them. Consider these factors:

- How loyal is the employee to the company?
- Is the employee happy with the culture?
- Are they happy with the environment?
- Do they agree with and heed the rules and regulations?
- Do they seem generally dissatisfied?
- How do they react to specific situations?
- Are they good communicators?
- Are they motivated or disengaged?

The answers to the questions above may speak volumes about selecting employees that can successfully handle the responsibility of cybersecurity issues.

Accountability and responsibility are important aspects of cybersecurity. When decisions are made with accountability and responsibility in mind, better decisions are made.

16: How to Address Security Threats

The first lines of defense against security threats are simple tasks. The key is to schedule and follow through with the tasks consistently to help protect your network and systems and prevent cyberattacks. You can schedule some of these tasks to run on computers and mobile devices without any further requirements from you. Others must be initiated by the user. Employees should be properly trained for carrying out these simple tasks.

Update Computers Regularly

Updating computers regularly is one of the most basic tasks to keep your computers, networks, and mobile devices up to date at all time. When software becomes obsolete, do not procrastinate with updates. When you see the popup for updates, update your software, firewall, web browsers, and antivirus immediately. When you ignore the update popups, you are making the hacker's job easy!

Utilize Anti-Virus and Anti-Malware Programs

For optimum computer and device performance, anti-virus and anti-malware programs are essential. You truly never know if an email contains a virus or if an attachment, even from a trusted source is infected and can infect or delete your files or wipe your hard drive. Recovering critical lost data can be very difficult or even impossible.

Cybercriminals are always busy developing software that is smarter than the current antivirus. If your software is out of date, you are leaving open a window for the cybercriminal.

Your computer becomes easy prey for the malicious intentions of the cybercriminal.

Passwords

It may seem elementary to think about passwords, but they are an integral part of any cybersecurity plan. Business managers must know how to select solid passwords and must teach their staff to do so.

One source says that if you select and keep passwords that can be easily found in the dictionary, hackers can gain access to your computer in less than 30 seconds. In *How to Devise Passwords that Drive Hackers Away,* author Nicole Perlroth says that passwords should be 14 letters long or more. Having a combination of upper-case and lower-case letters, along with symbols and numbers, makes the password more difficult to crack.

Since most people have difficulty remembering a long password, create one that you can easily remember but is not a common phrase or line of poetry, etc. Your password should be unique so that it is not easily searched as part of a famous movie line or such.

You should have a password for each website or online account that requires a password instead of using the same one for all sites and accounts. In other words, your email password, LinkedIn password, bank account password, and Facebook password should each be different. No two accounts should share the same password. Passwords should frequently be changed to keep cybercriminals from zeroing in and overtaking your account.

Yes, different passwords for each account and frequently changing passwords is a perfect formula for getting locked out of your accounts because you can't remember your password. That is easily remedied by purchasing a small, inexpensive password book where you can write down all your accounts and websites and the password and username for each. Make sure you update the password in the book each time you change it. Store the password book in a secure spot away from your computer desk.

Hire Competent Security Consultants

When you hire security consultants, check out their credentials and speak with them enough to make sure they understand what you require of them. At the very least, the competent security consultant should be able to find gaps within your system and make recommendations for solutions.

Train the Staff

Security breaches can occur because of mistakes made by your staff. It is imperative to cybersecurity for staff to be educated and trained regarding correct procedure for accessing information. Human error plays a significant part in security breaches.

Your staff should know about various types of cyberattacks and what makes your system vulnerable to attacks. They should know how to prevent attacks and what to do in the event of an attack.

Staff should be required to know the policies regarding cybersecurity. This includes whether they are allowed to access personal accounts and social media accounts from company computers and devices.

Limit Stored Data

When you no longer need sensitive data, transfer it to your backup or print and store somewhere else, but delete it from your computer. Disposing of data that is no longer needed makes you less of a target than computers that are loaded with confidential information.

VPN Service

With portable devices such as laptops and mobile phones, people carry around sensitive company data that can be easily stolen or lost, putting the sensitive data in the hands of someone who should not have it.

Additionally, with laptops and phones, users often use public WIFI that is not a secure internet connection. This makes your laptop or phone vulnerable to hacker attacks.

Since employees often use company laptops and phones in public places, the best solution is to choose a reputable VPN service provider, so the data remains protected even when an insecure WIFI connection is used. This protects the information that comes into and goes out of your device.

A VPN helps with encrypting your communications that take place over the internet, thus preventing leakage of information to a malicious party that might be tracking your movements.

These tasks are all basic, but they are often overlooked as part of an easy front-line defense against cyberattacks. Every business leader should practice these simple tasks and make sure the employees do also.

17: Cybersecurity for Mobile Devices

With the constant use of smartphones, tablets, and other smart devices, it is simple to access and transfer information from anywhere at any time. Unfortunately, along with this wonderful convenience comes the increase in security threats directed at cell phones. In fact, many malicious hackers purposely target cell phones because so many cell phones are left unprotected. This is not wise for company phones that have sensitive information on them.

Typical Attacks for Mobile Devices

Many of the threats for mobile devices are the same types that have been discussed regarding networks and databases on office computers, but some of the threats targeting mobile devices are more advanced. Because mobile devices are easy to carry around to different locations, the range of attacks differ from those faced by office business networks. Attackers have also modified their methods and are making use of the latest technology to hack into phones.

The most significant vulnerability of mobile phones is that they are so easily stolen or left behind by users at cafes, park benches, retail shops, the gym, and everywhere else people go on a frequent basis. With a lost or stolen phone, the attacker or thief can gain access to the personal and company information that is on the phone. Most business leaders do not pay much attention to all the critical information they carry on their phones. Even if the phone is equipped with security features, a sophisticated hacker, if given enough time with your device, can easily gain access to your information.

Cell phones also fall victim to malicious software that looks legitimate. People have a habit of downloading apps on their phones without a second thought to whether the app is legitimate and safe. People also bypass their cell phone's security network because it is inconvenient, they do not know how to use it, or they simply don't think their phone is vulnerable to viruses and attacks. This allows hackers to use legitimate or illegitimate apps to gain information from phones. The apps consist of bugs that are embedded into the files attached to the apps that, when downloaded, is installed on the mobile device. At that point, it is easy for the information to be transferred. This may be company security codes, banking information, sensitive proprietary information, passwords, and other information is transferred to cybercriminals with ill intentions.

Sometimes hackers embed your device with hardware that transmits your location and helps them gain access to your cell phone without you realizing it. The user may trigger this access by clicking on a malicious link that seems legitimate but is actually a way for the hacker to get into your system.

Phishing attacks are often used to make users click on links or download an app that contains malicious software. If the user knowingly or accidentally clicks the link, the intruder can enter the device with ease. Email phishing is one of the most common methods of attacking computers, and on mobile devices there are several ways to send links: SMS or MMS or even by voice call.

Phishing attacks are often targeted toward featured phones that are not equipped with the most advanced wireless or data capabilities. (This is a good reason for companies to update cell phones as frequently as they can!)

Sometimes, parties with malicious intent try to trick cell phone users into receiving fraudulent charges on their mobile phones. Phishing attacks often increase after a major event in the form of a new story with links for the reader to click.

Consequences of Ineffective Cyber Security for Mobile Devices

People often consider the security of their computers far more important than the security of their devices. They fail to remember that their smartphone is a computer! They also fail to consider all the confidential information that is on the phone. They may not carry around as many documents and files on their phone as they have on their office computer, but they are more likely to have more sensitive personal information on the phone or laptop than on the office computer. Additionally, it seems that people generally do not think their phone will reap the consequences of a cyberattack on their phone.

In days past, if one lost a cell phone, the only thing they had to worry about was the loss of their contact list. Now, people load their cell phones with all kinds of private information, and literally "carry their wallets" on their phone to pay for purchases with their phone. Many company employees carry company credit cards on their phone to use for traveling expenses or other work expenses. This is particularly true of business managers.

The consequences of a cyberattack that is targeted toward cell phones is just as severe as an attack on the office computer. Hackers can use the data and information on your cell phone in the same malicious ways they use the data and information on the office network.

Viruses can also enter mobile devices, and if the devices are connected to the office computer network, the malicious software can infiltrate the computer, jeopardizing financial records and critical confidential information. Usernames and passwords may also be lost, allowing cybercriminals to access all your accounts, including bank and credit accounts. Information that could harm a company's reputation could be leaked if an unauthorized phone search revealed the information.

How to Protect Mobile Devices

Security software for mobile devices is not always as sophisticated as that for computers, but there are steps you can take to protect your mobile devices. As a business leader, you should understand these steps and make sure your staff understands them.

1. **Select an appropriate mobile device that has security features**. Not all mobile devices are created equally when it comes to security features. Buy the device that comes equipped with software that offers ultimate security. Ask the service provider if the mobile phone has file encryption software. Ask whether the device can be wiped clean if required and whether it can detect and delete malicious software. Make sure the device contains authentication features where the screen and other data can be password protected. Most cell phones come with password or PIN protection. Some phones have software that shuts off the device if the device is reported stolen. When purchasing a phone, get all the security features you can.

2. **Take steps to configure the device so that it is protected.** The security features won't do you any good if you do not set them up and use them! Configure web accounts so they can only be

accessed through secure connections. Look for the HTTPS or the SSL in the account settings and enable the setting.

3. **Beware of spy bugs.** There are many variations of spy bugs that can be embedded in emails. It's best to only open emails from people that you know or companies that you trust. Do not click on links in emails. Copy the link and paste it into your browser instead.

4. **Limit your mobile device exposure.** In most companies, business leaders spend a lot of time on their mobile phones. It's part of any modern managerial position. It also makes the manager's phone vulnerable to attack due to the significant exposure of the phone number. It's best to give out your number to only your superiors, trusted co-workers, and business contacts so you can limit the exposure to fraudulent calls and messages. Keep a separate number for personal contacts, friends, and family.

5. **Know what information to keep in storage on your phone.** Before storing information on your phone, stop and think about the possible damage that could be done to the company if the phone with the information was lost or stolen and got into the wrong hands.

6. **Maintain physical control over your phone.** Whether you are in a meeting or out and about, keep your phone in a secure spot on your body, in your briefcase, or in your car. Don't leave your

phone where others can quickly grab it and run or where information on the phone can be seen by prying eyes. Don't leave it where it is likely that you will walk off without it.

7. **Turn off features.** When you can, leave your Bluetooth, infrared, and WIFI turned off when not in use. These features can be an open gateway for attackers. On your Bluetooth setting, make your device undiscoverable. This ensures that hackers cannot connect to your device through the Bluetooth feature.

8. **Don't use WIFI that is not secure.** Most business managers use their phones and devices in public places such as restaurants, airports, public meeting rooms, etc. Most places offer free WIFI, which saves data when on a limited data plan. However, unknown or public WIFI makes your phone vulnerable for others to gain access to the information on your phone.

9. **Take precautions when you discard the device.** When it's time to get a new phone, carefully discard or pass on the old phone. Be aware that even when data is deleted, it can be recovered by a hacker. Delete all data, including data stored on the memory card. Refer to the phone manufacturer's instruction for wiping the phone clean in a secure manner.

10. **Take precautions when using social network sites.** Social media sites can be entertaining and keep you in touch with friends and family. But they are also a playground for cybercriminals. Go to the site's

settings page and set the most stringent security you can regarding who can see your information and location.

11. **Jailbreak is not a good idea.** Many people use Jailbreak so they can access the apps that are not presently in their cell phone's store. This is definitely not a good idea because the phone becomes vulnerable to external attacks. Most of the apps are locked by default because they are thought to contain malicious codes that are designed to attack your mobile phone. It also prevents your phone from receiving software updates that can be critical for the protection of confidential information.

12. **Avoid mobile malware by being a careful user of the device.** There are many threats posed by mobile malware. Among the threats are social networking exploitation, social engineering, mobile application exploitation, mobile botnets, and M-Commerce. Always take the precautions mentioned above and adopt the policy of erring on the safe side when you are uncertain about anything in your email or on your phone that seems suspicious.

If Your Mobile Device is Stolen

Mobile devices are hot-theft items because they are easily used by the thief or sold. They also contain information that the thief can use for malicious purposes. Because mobile devices are so easily stolen or lost, it's important to backup all information. Many cell phone companies provide backup service and space in the cloud for backing up information that can be retrieved if the phone is stolen or lost and put back on the new phone. If you do not use this service, choose another backup.

If your mobile device is stolen, take quick action; don't procrastinate. Report your stolen or lost phone to the authorities. It is likely that the authorities will do nothing to recover the phone, but you may need the police report to file an insurance report to have your phone replaced.

Report your phone stolen to your service provider. Often, they have good advice on what you can do next to secure your phone to minimize the damage caused by thieves.

If your phone is a company phone, report the stolen phone to the appropriate department and be prepared to provide them with the type of company information on the phone that has become compromised. Follow the company policy.

Change your account credentials for accessing financial accounts such as online banking or credit cards. When appropriate to do so, place holds on debit or credit cards if you believe the thief can access those card numbers from your phone.

Some mobile service providers have excellent anti-theft features that allow them to remotely lock your phone or wipe it clean so the thief can't access your information. Make sure you know your provider's provision for this ahead of time.

If you take all the precautions listed in this chapter, you can keep your mobile device secure and enjoy the advantages of portable devices without experiencing the darker side of cybercrime.

It's also important for the business leader to have their staff trained and educated regarding mobile devices. When employees access the company's network through their personal devices or the company's mobile devices, the network becomes vulnerable to external and internal threats.

Business leaders must keep a tab on which company devices are in use and by whom and what information each individual accesses with the device. This may be easier said than done, but it's the responsibility of the manager to set systems in place to monitor employee's use of company devices unless the IT department takes on that responsibility. Even then, the manager needs to keep a finger on the pulse of mobile device security.

18: Common Cybersecurity Mistakes

As with everything else in business, the business manager will learn more about cybersecurity as they go. The important thing is to learn as quickly as you can to avoid costly and time-consuming mistakes. Your IT department or professional can be very helpful in sharing their knowledge and expertise with you.

Some leaders prefer to outsource cybersecurity because they know their time limitations and skill set does not permit them to fully address cybersecurity in a way that is best for the business. Nonetheless, as has been well established in this guide, the business leader needs to know enough about cybersecurity to keep their employees and business protected. In this chapter, you'll find some of the most common cybersecurity mistakes and how to avoid them.

Mistake #1: The Goal is to Achieve 100% Security

In many organizations, the objective is to attain 100% cybersecurity. The problem is that 100% security is an unattainable and unrealistic approach to solving the issues surrounding cybersecurity. Implementing effective security is important, but there is always an inherent risk.

Whether the cybersecurity practices of a business are private or made public by company officials, every organization faces risks on a regular basis no matter how many preventive steps are taken to prevent network breaches, information theft, and intrusions. The cybersecurity climate is an ever-changing one, making it impossible to maintain 100% security at all times. Rather, the goal is to create defensive strategies with an emphasis on prevention. Additionally, use the best software and tools possible, make informed cybersecurity decisions, train the staff, remain diligent, and understand how to recover when there is an incident.

Mistake #2: Investing in the Best Technology Means Effective Cyber Security

As in any industry, the cybersecurity world is chock full of specialist and suppliers with technical products that allow the detection and elimination of intruders. Quality tools and the expertise of specialists are critical and should be integrated into your system. However, these technological systems should not be relied upon to form the basis of a robust and all-inclusive cybersecurity policy.

It is imperative that business leaders understand that by simply using and integrating these tools, optimal effectiveness may not be achieved. Investment in the tools must be viewed as output and not the driver of the cybersecurity strategic framework.

Good security for any system begins with the development of a strong cybersecurity strategy that encompasses all the defensive capabilities of the system. This is where a specialist can be of benefit to you. The most critical and comprehensive steps should be carried out by the cybersecurity specialist. The business leader, however, should understand what is being implemented and what their role is in the process and monitoring of cybersecurity. It is also the responsibility of the manager to make sure the staff is trained according to the specialist's specifications for optimal cybersecurity.

Mistake #3: Our Technological Weapons Should Be Better than the Attackers

Warring with cybercriminals is a never-ending war. Hackers and malicious parties are always looking for and designing new and improved software and methods by which they can attack your system. The defense (you and your business) is always a step or more behind. Frustrating? Yes, of course it is frustrating. But the fact is that you could work on nothing but cybersecurity 24 hours per day, and you would still have vulnerabilities in your system.

That said, do your best! Keep your systems updated with the latest software, learn as much as you can reasonably learn from your IT department or professional, remain aware and diligent and train your staff. Know your enemy. Prioritize and identify your vulnerabilities. Know your most valuable core assets and initiate policies that strongly protect the most critical assets of the company. Rather than fret and worry about it, use a flexible approach that proactively and strategically addresses the issues.

Mistake #4: Effective Monitoring Leads to Cybersecurity Compliance

Most business leaders focus on monitoring effectively whether or not their business's security strategy and implementation complies with the cybersecurity protocols they have implemented. While monitoring the system always is important, the ability to learn from any mistakes or successful breaches is equally important.

Cybersecurity is, no doubt, driven by compliance. The organization must keep pace with the laws and legislation requirements of cybersecurity for the industry. However, holding compliance as the ultimate goal of cybersecurity is counterproductive. Eventually, the organizations that are successful in combatting the cyber threats and crime are those capable of understanding how the development in the environment and emerging trends will affect their company. In other words, compliance alone is not efficient for cybersecurity.

It's important for all businesses to learn and develop continuously to ensure future growth. It is no different when it comes to cybersecurity. Compliance rules may remain the same, but the company may need to move forward with updated, advanced strategies for combatting cybercrime. A business leader should keep his or her finger on the pulse of emerging trends and the evolution of threats in the cybersecurity world. This leads to the development of effective network security changes.

Mistake #5: Recruiting the Best Professionals Will Keep the Business Safe from Cyber Crime

Depending on the structure and size of the business, in many, a single department or specialist handles the organization's cybersecurity. However, in this guide, you have realized that the business leader and employees also play a large role in the cybersecurity of the business. The manager and employees bear some responsibility for cybersecurity and must not develop the attitude that caution can be thrown to the wind because *it's the IT department or person's job.* This mentality results in a false sense of security for the business. The IT person or department is counting on the manager and employees to do their part.

Cybersecurity is an organization-wide issue. HR policies must be implemented regarding security protocols and rules. The staff must realize the importance of their tasks and mindset regarding cybersecurity. If they do not, the best IT team in the world won't be effective.

Conclusion

Even as this book is being written, the importance of cybersecurity in today's world is increasing at an alarming rate. Every business leader must be aware of its strategic use and conformity with the overall objectives of the business.

The author of the book has tried to emphasize the need for all business leaders to focus, not only on branding and creating new products for the profitability of the company, but also on the securing company information so the company and its leaders and employees can enjoy the fruit of their labor without the intrusion and devastation of severe cybercrime.

About the Author
Mr. Derek Smith, CISSP, MBA, MS, Speaker, Author, and Educator

Derek A. Smith is the founder of the National Cybersecurity Education Center and is responsible for the development and coordination of cybersecurity initiatives at the Center. Formerly he was the Director of Cybersecurity Initiatives at the National Cybersecurity Institute at Excelsior College. Derek has worked for the federal government as a federal agent, cybersecurity manager, and IT program manager. He has also worked for several IT companies including Computer Sciences Corporation and Booz Allen Hamilton.

Derek regularly appears on various news programs as a cyber security expert and conducts regular webinars, podcasts, and blogs, and public talks.

Derek is an associate professor at the University of Maryland, University College, Virginia University of Science and Technology and Excelsior College and has taught business and cyber classes for over 25 years. He is also a Board advisor for several boards.

Derek served in the US Navy, Air Force, and Army for a total of 24 years. He has completed an MBA, MS in Digital Forensics, MS in IT Information Assurance, Masters in IT Project Management, and a B.S in Education. Derek also completed all but the dissertation for a Doctorate of Education degree in Organizational Leadership and Conflict and Dispute Resolution.

For fun, Derek has practiced martial arts for over 35 years and hold black belts in several martial arts. He also has acted in movies, television, industrial films, and commercials. Derek is available for consulting, training, and speaking engagements. You can contact him at the National Cybersecurity Education Center at derek@ncseconline.com

Derek lives with his family in Bowie, Maryland. More information about Derek is available at www.Derekallensmith.net.

www.ingramcontent.com/pod-product-compliance
Lightning Source LLC
Chambersburg PA
CBHW071004050326
40689CB00014B/3492